M

Knowing Who You Are in
Christ Changes Everything

Amy Holmes

Crest Publishers
P.O. Box 595 •
Chelsea, Alabama 35043

To my best friend, Jesus

Thank You, Lord, for giving me the desire
of my heart.

How I love You!

Prologue

"Jesus knows me, this I love." *–Unknown*

For as long as I can remember I have wanted to write a book. During my Nancy Drew and Trixie Belden phases in elementary school, I tried my literary hand at mysteries. Then I moved on to teen romances during my Sweet Valley High phase in junior high. My biggest problem was that I had no experience with either topic. I had never solved a mystery, and I certainly had no experience in the romance department. To this day, my great novels sit unfinished in notebooks that have long been recycled.

As a teacher, I have learned and now teach my students that you write what you know. Four years ago I couldn't have written anything about the exciting subject I want to share with you in the following pages. I simply didn't know enough about the subject matter, and my perception of Him was largely incorrect. Today I can write with confidence about Him—Jesus, that is—because I know Him, and my understanding and my confidence have been built on the foundation of who He is and who I am in Him!

In November of 2015, God fulfilled one of my fondest dreams. My husband, Mike, and I traveled to Israel for an 11-day journey into the land of the

Bible. It was a life-changing experience for both of us as we walked where our Savior and so many heroes of the faith have walked. We stood on Mt. Carmel, sailed across the Sea of Galilee, were baptized in the Jordan River, toured the Temple Mount in Jerusalem, prayed at the Garden of Gethsemane, and rejoiced in the empty tomb. The day before we left on our trip was my 46th birthday. On my way to church that morning, I was listening to Chris Tomlin's "Good, Good Father" for the umpteenth time. It had been on repeat for quite awhile in my car. As I rode along and sang about who my Father is (He's good) and who I am (loved greatly by Him), He gave me the most wonderful birthday gift I've ever received. He dropped the idea for this book into my spirit. I had been seeking Him for some time about how I might help other people by sharing my journey in Him, and this was my answer.

The next day I listened to "Good, Good Father" for the majority of our ten-hour flight to Tel Aviv. When we hit the ground, I listened to it all over Israel, and it became the anthem for this book. My Heavenly Father's identity is that He is a very good Father. My identity in Him is that I am loved by Him. It is who I am.

Reading from the book of Haggai recently, I noticed that the author named two men specifically—Zerubbabel, son of Shealtiel, and Jeshua, son of Jehozadak. Many times the Bible identifies people by who their fathers are. And so it is with us who are born again. Our identity is based in Jesus and in who our Father is. Now that's good news!

Identity is everything. In order to know where we're going, what we have, and what is possible on life's journey, we must first know who we are. "Oh, that's easy!" we might say. After all, we see ourselves in the mirror every day. We make decisions that determine the course of our days and the way our relationships will go. We know our past and all the secret thoughts that no one else knows we have. We have been with ourselves every moment since conception. How could we not know our own selves? Who could possibly know us better than we? In truth, we may not know who we are at all. And in absolute truth, there is One who knows us better than anyone else in the universe, including ourselves.

For 25 of my 29 years as a Christian, I had absolutely no idea who I was. A few years ago, our former worship pastor had a favorite song, and when I heard the initial chords (almost weekly there for a while), I would feel irritation prickle my nerves. "I Know Who I Am"—*really*?? What a dumb song! I hate this song! These were my thoughts each time we sang it. My apologies to the composer and to our worship leader. Even though the song gave me obvious answers, I was still clueless. My irritation stemmed from not knowing my true identity in Christ. I didn't know who I was because I really didn't know who Jesus is or what His finished work on the cross had accomplished for me.

Oh, but thank God for my dear friend Helene Catalano who, in the summer of 2012, introduced me to teachings about the gospel of grace by Pastor Joseph Prince. These teachings literally revolutionized the way I saw myself and the way I understood and knew Jesus and His finished work. I am a life changed by the grace of God. And that grace is a Person. His name is Jesus Christ. My prayer for you, dear reader, is that you, too, will come to know who He truly is. And in finding Him, you will find yourself!

Chapter 1—*My Story Part 1*

My story begins before I can even remember. My earliest memories are of trying to do my best to make sure everyone around me thought that I was the sweetest, most wonderful person they had ever had the joy of knowing. My earliest memories also include sexual abuse at the hands of a family friend, which robbed me of innocence and evoked fear, shame, self consciousness, and an intense desire to please people. I felt so poorly about myself that I would do anything to please others and momentarily achieve the worth and value that I craved.

I was raised in church, and at the tender age of eight, I decided to follow Jesus. . .into the baptistery, that is. That was my one and only goal. Some other kids my age were beginning to make decisions to follow Jesus as their Savior, but my main reason for making my way into my pastor's office to pray the prayer was to venture into the baptistery, not into a life given over to Jesus. I can't even recall what I prayed that day, but those aquamarine waves gently lapping at the glass front of the baptistery high up in the choir loft of Cahaba Heights Baptist Church mesmerized me, and I had to experience them for myself. I know that Jesus understood my eight-year-old heart, but for years I felt great distress inside knowing that I wasn't "truly saved."

I doubted my salvation throughout my childhood until I answered the altar call at youth camp in March of 1987. The evangelist preached on seven points of salvation. I could say yes to none, and felt the Spirit tugging at my heart. I walked the aisle of the chapel at Shocco Springs Baptist Conference Center and gave my heart to Jesus, knowing that this time it was for real.

I had gotten into major trouble the weekend before, which resulted in my all-expense paid trip to youth camp over spring break. My mother was making her point clear. Straighten up and pronto! And I'm so thankful she did. Despite my initial angst at the mandatory trip, my life really did change after I received Jesus. . .for a little while anyway. I sincerely asked Him into my heart that evening in March of 1987, but I was under the grand delusion that asking Jesus into my heart was the end-all to my experience with and need for Him.

Initially, I thought that I could do what I wanted when I wanted and just ask forgiveness, but when I did, I felt such guilt and shame. I really had no idea that asking Jesus into my heart was only the beginning of an eternal journey, and I had no clue how to grow in the Lord. I was under the dangerous belief that my works and my confession of sins would make me right with God. I believed that Jesus had died for my sins, but I adhered to the very misguided notion that it was now up to me to carry out the rest of my salvation. I lived a defeated life, laboring under that misconception until June of 2012.

Even though Jesus said, "It is finished!" (John 19:30[1]) when He hung on the cross, I had no idea that meant that the work Jesus did on the cross is a *finished* work. There is nothing I can add to it with my actions or take away from it with my actions.

Until the summer of 2012, I had based my Christian identity on my own efforts; and to tell you the truth, I really didn't know who in the world I was. I was a chameleon, changing my color to that of my surroundings. Whatever you liked, I loved if I was with you. If you didn't like it, I backpedaled my way out of liking it, too. Bless my husband's heart! He was not a believer when we married and had no idea he'd married a Christian until he found some 4Him tapes hidden in the console of our Z24. I wasn't living like a Christian when I met him, and I was afraid for him to see that side of me. I was one mixed-up mess!

But thank God! He specializes in making miracles out of messes. And I was no surprise to Him. Four years ago, He began to teach me things I had no

---

[1] Unless otherwise indicated, all Scripture references used in this book are from the New Living Translation.

idea about, and it was like unraveling knots in a beautiful necklace. The beauty was there, just all wound up around itself and unable to be useful to the wearer or to be seen by others. The beauty of the necklace is not me by the way. The beauty is Jesus. My misguided beliefs were the metaphoric knots that He began to unravel by His glorious grace. And I am so in love with Him for it!

In order to go forward in my understanding of and relationship with Him, I had to go back—back to the beginning. Back to where mankind's identity crisis began. Back to a beautiful garden where our God-given identity was stolen.

The Garden of Eden was paradise indeed. The landscape was enough to qualify it as such, but God's presence, devotion to, and relationship with Adam and Eve were the components that truly qualified the garden as paradise. Adam and Eve walked in unbroken face-to-face fellowship with God their Creator. I like to imagine them on picnics and long walks in the most beautiful settings, laughing together and deeply enjoying each other's company. That was the desire of our Father's heart—to have a family that loved Him by choice, not by compulsion. Thus He placed the tree of the knowledge of good and evil in the garden (Genesis 2 AMP). He wanted Adam and Eve to choose Him, but in so desiring, He had to give them a choice. And sadly, they chose poorly, and they chose for all of us. Eve allowed herself to doubt God's identity, to doubt His heart. Satan cleverly attacked God's character. Why would God put such a tree there unless He was trying to keep Adam and Eve from something that would be wonderful? Satan made Eve doubt God's motives, and in so doing, she doubted who God really is. She allowed herself to be deceived, and Adam followed suit. And so began the corrupted misconception of the true identity of our Father and ourselves (Genesis 3 AMP).

This is the point where I used to have a big problem. Why didn't God just say, "Oh, it's okay. I know you feel really guilty. I'll take care of everything," instead of making them leave Eden? Why didn't He just let it go—forgive and forget? The reason shows the steadfast, perfect love only our Heavenly Father can possess. He had also planted another tree in the garden—the tree of life—and He knew that if Adam and Eve ate from that tree in their fallen state, there would be no hope of redemption for them or for us. They would live forever. . .fallen (Gen. 3:22 AMP). He couldn't abide the thought, so He banished them from the garden. Before doing so, He made the first sacrifice by killing an animal to cover them. Life is in the blood, and the blood of an innocent had to be shed to cover their sin, whose wage is death (Romans 6:23). The skin of an animal now covered them instead of the glory of God that had clothed them before. God also placed angels at the garden entrances and a flaming sword before the tree of life to ensure that they could not eat of it. You see,

He had already created a plan before the foundation of the world to redeem mankind, to buy back our stolen identity. He would do it Himself, because He loves us that much (1 Peter 1:20, Rev. 13:8).

To me, this is the area in which Satan always begins his attack. He wants us to doubt God's character and His love for us, and doubt breeds fear. If he can make us discount God's love and believe the lie that He is out to get us, Satan can keep us afraid and defeated. He can keep us weak. But once we know that God loves us perfectly, we will have no fear (1 John 4:18). And when we have no fear, we see God for who He really is, and we can trust Him implicitly. When that type of faith is produced in our hearts, born of the Father's love for us, nothing will be impossible for us!

When Adam disobeyed God and ate the forbidden fruit, he handed Satan the dominion and authority that had been given to him (Gen. 1:27-28). The devil has been using it against the human race ever since. But our wonderful God in His infinite wisdom knew all of this would occur before He even created the world. Isaiah 46:10 assures us that He truly does know the end from the beginning: "Declaring the end from the beginning, and from ancient times *the things* that are not *yet* done, saying, 'My counsel shall stand, and I will do all my pleasure. . .'" (KJV) His pleasure was to send His one and only precious Son to be born of a virgin; to live a perfect, sinless life; and to give His life as a ransom for many (Mark 10:45). Though He was the King of the universe, the Lord of all creation, He *chose* to come down to His creation and become a servant of all to show us how to live victoriously. As a child and as a man, Jesus had no problem submitting to authority. He had no issues with serving others because He *knew* from the depths of His being *who He is* and *whose He is.* He was secure in His Father's love for Him.

Jesus was the first man—yes, He is fully man and fully God—who did not have an identity crisis. He *knew* His Father! Oh, friend, if we know who our Father is, we too will know who we are and live in victory over every wile of the enemy. We know the Father through knowing Jesus. When He walked on earth, He was the visible, tangible image of God Almighty. In seeing Jesus, we see the Father (John 14:7-10).

For most of my life, I had an image of God as a harsh and hard-to-please taskmaster. I was so afraid that if I stepped out of line an inch He would be waiting to come down with His sledgehammer of judgment and that it was my obedience or lack thereof that determined my standing with Him. I didn't trust Him because I didn't love Him. I didn't love Him because I didn't know how very much He loves me! My distrust led me, like Eve back in Genesis, to doubt His character. My view of God as judge opened doors of misconception about how

He really feels about me and about all people. It ultimately led me to doubt my salvation for most of my Christian life. If you believe as I did that your standing with God is based on what you have done rather than what Jesus has done for you on the cross, you too will live a defeated, doubtful life never really knowing where you stand with Him.

When I depended on my own effort, I could be in and out of fellowship with God a hundred times in the course of a day. I perceived my standing with Him was based on my performance. If I was minding my manners, praying and reading my Bible for a certain amount of time, no matter if I understood it or focused on it, then I could expect great things from God. Oh, reader, are you there? Are you living an unsure existence in that shaky house built on the sandy foundation of your works making you right with God? I know right where you are! I held the deed to that miserable piece of real estate my whole Christian life. . .until the depths of one balmy July night in 2012.

For several weeks, I had been listening to teachings on grace by Pastor Joseph Prince of New Creation Church in Singapore. At first the things he taught seemed too good to be true. They were amazing, and my spirit lifted at hearing such revelations of Jesus and His finished work. Afraid that I might be heading down the wrong road, I began to follow along in my Bible during every televised sermon. I would look up each thing Pastor Prince taught to ensure its validity. I researched every Scripture he shared, and they said EXACTLY what he said they did.

On that particular night in July, I could not sleep. My family was dealing with issues, and sleep evaded me. I finally got out of bed and went to another room and found Pastor Prince on YouTube. I was enjoying a worship song by his team called "I See Grace." I began to worship Jesus in my heart along with them. Pastor Prince came up to give an exhortation to the congregation, and the words he spoke became living words to me. He said something like this, "He who knew no sin became sin for us so that we could become the righteousness of God in Christ Jesus. If perfect Jesus could become sin for us, then we can become righteous in Him." (2 Corinthians 5:21) An electric shock went off in my heart, and a divine understanding unfolded! Jesus is perfect. He knows no sin, but His finished work on the cross encompassed becoming sin so that I could become righteous in Him! He not only covered my sin, He washed it away completely. Annihilated it! Destroyed it! Completely exonerated me in every way before God and gave me His identity with the Father! Oh, friend, if that makes you shout for joy, it gets better. Not only did He cleanse me of past sins, He cleansed me of ALL sins-past, present, and future! I have to stop and shout here, too! Praise You, Jesus! That revelation never ceases to bless my heart. It drives out fear and brings such security. And security brings freedom!

When we mix our right standing with God based on our behavior (law) and our right standing with God based on Jesus' finished work on the cross (grace-God's unearned, unmerited favor), it's like mixing oil and water. The two will never combine. The Bible was very confusing to me at times, but when I began to see the difference between law and grace, and what the two really are, it all became so clear.

Jesus said,

> Besides, who would patch old clothing with new cloth? For the new patch would shrink and rip away from the old cloth, leaving an even bigger tear than before. And no one puts new wine into old wineskins. For the old skins would burst from the pressure, spilling the wine and ruining the skins. New wine is stored in new wineskins so that both are preserved. (Matthew 9:16-17)

I always wondered what in the world that meant for me. I believe Jesus was telling us that the old covenant of law given through Moses cannot mix with the new covenant of grace which came through Jesus Himself. The law was given to show that we cannot keep it. It is perfect and good and holy, but I am not. Without Jesus, I am incapable of

doing what is right. He alone is my righteousness.
My standing with God is not based on me or my
behavior. It is solely based on Jesus and His
finished work on the cross. Praise the name of
Jesus through endless ages! Friend, we have just
begun. It only gets better from here!

Chapter 2—*Gideon's Story*

As we have ascertained through Adam and Eve's story, identity has been an issue from almost the beginning of time. Long before I burst onto the scene in 1969 anyway. Have you ever just thought about that? About how many people have entered and exited our planet since its creation? And they are all in eternity. . .somewhere. Either with our Father in Heaven or in an eternal hell forever separated from Him. Jesus gave His life so that we could have eternal life with Him. My prayer is that if you don't already know Him as your Savior, that you will before you turn the last page of this book.

Centuries before Jesus came in the flesh, there lived a man named Gideon. Under the old covenant of law, Gideon lived before Israel ever had a human king, before they demanded a king like all of their pagan neighbors had (1 Samuel 8). In the natural, having a king may sound like a good thing for the nation of Israel. But God was their king! Who could ask for more? Friend, don't we do the same type of thing all the time? I try not to be too critical of the nonsensical things that people in the Bible do, because I think I might be right in there with them in some instances. Before I understood that Christ is my wisdom, holiness, righteousness, and redemption (I Corinthians 1:30), I had so many wrong beliefs about God and did innumerable dumb things myself. It has taken some time to "unlearn" them all, and I'm still in the growth process. But I am so excited about what I know about the Lord and how I know Him now, that I am committing these things to print in hopes that you too will come to this understanding and that it will change your life!

Let's get back to our friend Gideon, whose story can be found in Judges 6. As we delve into it, we can infer a few things about him. He was fearful, insecure, and doubtful. When we meet Gideon, he is hiding in a winepress and threshing wheat there. He is trying to separate the wheat from the chaff in an enclosure meant to expel juice from grapes, which must be a very difficult task. In order to thresh properly, one must use a winnowing fork to toss the wheat high into the air to separate it from the chaff. Gideon is down in the winepress so that the Midianites won't see him (fear). The Midianites were a people group in the land of Canaan who had been raiding Israel's land and stripping it bare. The children of Israel cried out to God for help, and because He is a wonderful God full of mercy and loving kindness, He listened and was moved to action.

Now God sees Gideon down in the winepress and sends the Angel of the Lord to give him the plan for Israel's rescue. Gideon has several arguments to disqualify himself from leading this important mission. Undoubtedly, he has rehearsed these things about himself his whole life. Like so many of us, he is looking at himself and his abilities rather than at God and His unsurpassable ability.

The Angel's greeting is quite the opposite of what Gideon would say about himself. "Mighty hero, the Lord is with you!" (Judges 6:12) What? Huh? Who, me? I can just see Gideon with an astonished, scrunched-up face, mouth ajar, pointing to himself and mouthing "Me?" in disbelief. He probably looks around to see if the Angel is really talking to him. The Angel of the Lord goes on to say, "Go with the strength you have, and rescue Israel from the Midianites. I am sending you!" (Judges 6:14)

When Gideon realizes that it is indeed he to whom the Angel is speaking, this is what the "mighty hero" says: "O my Lord, how can I save Israel? Indeed my clan *is* the weakest in Manasseh, and I *am* the least in my father's house." (Insecurity.) (Judges 6:15 NKJV)

Oh, my friend, Gideon is doing what you and I so often do. He hears only what the Angel says about him, and it just doesn't ring true in his heart because of his identity crisis. I'm sure he is thinking about going in the strength *he* has to rescue Israel and he totally misses that God is the One sending Him! He is looking at *his own* abilities and depending on *his own* strength. Can he in his natural strength rescue Israel from the Midianites?

Absolutely, positively not! All he hears is "mighty hero" and "go with the strength you have, and rescue Israel." His self-doubt deafens him to the most important parts: "The Lord is with you," and "I (the Lord) am sending you." The Lord will enable Gideon to do exploits beyond his wildest imagination and his natural ability. If he'll just get on board with what God says about him, Gideon will be unstoppable.

The Angel of the Lord goes on to say, "I will be with you. And you will destroy the Midianites as if you were fighting against one man." (Judges 6:16) When I read these words, I see the Lord putting his "super" on Gideon's "natural"! If we will go when he says go and trust that He's the One who will fight our battles for us, we will experience the supernatural.

Gideon had a major case of mistaken identity. He only saw himself as Gideon, the least of the least. He didn't initially see himself as God's chosen warrior of the hour, but when he allowed himself to trust God (after a few tests to make sure it was God—doubt), God did mighty things through him. Gideon was the vessel God chose to show His awesome power through. The same is true of we who are in Christ. We are simply the vessel He works through. It's His ability and His wisdom that enable us to live the life He died to give us. Jesus gives us both the power and the desire to do His will (Philippians 2:13). When we approach life from

a place of resting in Christ and depending on His
ability in us instead of trying to do God's will and
be who He's called us to be in our own strength,
we will walk in freedom and victory. We CANNOT
live the Christian life without Christ being our
enabler! He gives us the ability and even the want-
to when we lay our efforts down and depend solely
on Him and His finished work at the cross.

Gideon went on to defeat the Midianites with a
very small army and in a way that only God can
orchestrate. The wonderful thing is that God
received all the glory, because Gideon knew that it
had absolutely nothing to do with his ability.

It's the same with us, except we are so much more
privileged than Gideon! We now have the Spirit of
God abiding *within* us if we are born again, and we
can talk to Him and worship Him in a very personal
way. We can come boldly to the throne of grace to
receive mercy and help in our time of need
(Hebrews 4:16). And it's all because of Jesus, the
perfect Son of God, who forged a path to our
Father with His own precious blood. It is only by His
blood and by His finished work on the cross that we
can call God Father and enter into His presence
without reservation.

When Gideon trusted God and believed what God
said about him, he was victorious. The same is true
for you and for me!

Chapter 3—*Mephibosheth's Story*

Another person that comes to mind when I think of mistaken identity is Mephibosheth, the son of Jonathan and grandson of Israel's first king, Saul. Mephibosheth, too, lived under the old covenant of law. In order to fully understand his story, we must know where he came from. His grandfather, King Saul, had had a myriad of problems, which affected his entire family. King Saul placed his own desires above God's directives and his need to please the people above his need to please God, which ultimately led to his demise (1 Samuel 15:20-34).

King Saul's son Jonathan had a different heart than his father. In fact, Jonathan had a special bond with a young warrior named David, who would become Saul's successor. God had chosen David, a shepherd boy turned valiant warrior, to take Saul's place. Because the people loved David, Saul developed an intense hatred for him that led to numerous attempts on David's life. Jonathan had such a bond with his best friend David that he intervened to save him, even though he knew it would cost him the throne. Jonathan and David cut a covenant, which meant that they would take care of each other and each other's families come what may (I Samuel 18).

After Saul and Jonathan were killed in battle (I Samuel 31), David was anointed king of Israel (2 Samuel 2). When word reached the palace that Saul and Jonathan were dead, panic ensued. Jonathan's young son Mephibosheth was dropped by his nurse as she fled the palace. As a result, he was crippled (2 Samuel 4:4).

The next time we hear of Mephibosheth, he is grown and living in a place called Lo-Debar, which just sounds depressing. And apparently it was. Lo-Debar means "without pasture" (biblestudytools.com), which to me, indicates a place of wondering with no sustenance or rest. Here in this place of unrest, Mephibosheth, once the grandson of a king and in line for the throne himself, lived lame in both feet.

He had been a small child when his father and grandfather had died, so perhaps he never really knew what his future should have held aside from renderings of those around him. He may have lived in fear that if he were found, David, who was now Israel's king, would kill him. Historically, kings had inclinations of that sort when an heir-apparent survived. But David remembered his covenant with his deceased friend and sought out anyone who might have survived from Saul's household in order to show kindness to them for Jonathan's sake (2 Samuel 9:4).

Can you imagine Mephibosheth's reaction when he was summoned by King David? It may have been much like that of our friend in Gideon in the previous chapter. I am sure his reaction was also tinged with fear. We see just how low his self esteem was in 2 Samuel 9:5-8. When he arrived at the palace, he bowed in respect to King David and declared that he was David's servant. Perhaps his humility was genuine or might have been born out of fear. Either way, David reassured him and told him not to be afraid, that he only wanted to bless him and show him kindness for the sake of his father, Jonathan. Mephibosheth must have been floored! We can assume that he thought he was done for when David summoned him, and yet David blessed him immensely, just as our King does for us. So often we think that God is hunting us down in order to punish us. In truth, it's just the opposite. We have a covenant—an eternal promise—cut in the blood of His Son, and our Father—our King—is hunting us down to bless us! That's such good news! When we are in Christ, God is our Father, and all of His promises belong to us. We find ourselves in Christ when we are born again. We are born again by confessing with our mouth that Jesus is Lord and believing in our hearts that God has raised Him from the dead (Romans 10:9). It's that simple! When we are in Christ, He becomes our identity. When I finally understood this, my insecurities melted away. And believe you me, I was one of the worst cases you've ever seen!

I wouldn't even call for takeout or ask for help in a store. I had to be as invisible as possible at all times.

We catch another glimpse of Mephibosheth's self loathing in 2 Samuel 9:8. Mephibosheth said, "Who is your servant, that you should show such kindness to *a dead dog like me?*" (Emphasis mine) Now that is a severe misconception of oneself! I was definitely afraid to make phone calls and go shopping alone, but I don't think I ever thought of myself as a dead dog.

King David didn't even respond to that. He simply called in a man named Ziba and told him all that he had given Mephibosheth, which was everything that belonged to Saul and his family. He directed Ziba and his sons to care for all of Mephibosheth's newly acquired land and then directed Mephibosheth to eat at his very own table with him. Do you see that? David said that Mephibosheth was to eat *at* his table, not *under* it! David let that whole "dead dog" comment go right by him. He focused on his covenant with Jonathan and all that belonged to Mephibosheth because of it. Do you also see that Mephibosheth didn't even have to work (produce something in his own effort) the land given him? This is another picture of our covenant with our Father through Jesus. Our Father shows us His kindness for Jesus' sake, blesses us with an inheritance in Him, and we don't even have to work for it! It cannot be earned. It's by His grace. Now, please don't misunderstand me. That doesn't mean we should just lie back and let the world pass us by because Jesus has done the work. Yes, He absolutely has, but when we are in Him, abiding in Him, we *want* to be productive for His glory. Jesus truly does give us both the power and the desire to do His good pleasure when we are abiding in Him!

Chapter 4—*Peter's Story*

I must admit that I struggled a bit with this chapter because I initially didn't understand the Lord's leading in its inclusion in a book about mistaken identity. Then it dawned on me that Peter's wasn't necessarily a case of *mistaken* identity but of a *radically changed* identity, which is what occurs in all of us once we have had an encounter with Jesus and His irresistible grace. It is His unearned, unmerited favor, and it draws us to Him and changes us into His image.

Peter had the unique experience of living under both the old covenant of law and the new covenant of grace. When we first meet him in the gospels, his name is Simon, and he is a rugged fisherman who works with his father, Jonah, and his brother Andrew. Historians identify him and his brother Andrew as followers of John the Baptist, which indicates that God was already preparing their hearts before they met Jesus. John foretold of Messiah's coming when he said,

> Someone is coming soon who is greater than I am—so much greater that I'm not even worthy to stoop down like a slave and untie the straps of his sandals. I baptize you with water, but he will

baptize you with the Holy Spirit! (Mark 1:7-8)

Can you just imagine the scene when Jesus called Peter and his brother out of obscurity and into a brotherhood that would literally change the world for all time? I can see the hot Galilean sun shimmering on the blue waters of the Sea of the Galilee as the brothers hoisted their net and cast it into the depths. They heard a voice calling with a timbre like none they'd ever heard before. There was a hint of eternity and Heaven's glory in that voice that made it distinct, authoritative, and gentle all at once. "Come, follow me, and I will show you how to fish for people!" (Mark 1:17) Peter, who was still known as Simon at that time, and Andrew dropped that heavy net and immediately followed Jesus. They left the family business, all of their equipment, and their livelihood to follow the One who had promised to show them how to catch people.

In the gospel of Luke, we find our first real hint of Simon Peter's feelings about himself. In Luke chapter 5, we see that great crowds began to assemble whenever Jesus was near. Jesus spied two empty fishing boats, one of which belonged to Peter, stepped into it, and asked Peter to push it out into the water so that He could speak to the people from there. That vantage point would amplify his voice and allow all the people to see Him. When Jesus finished speaking, He told Peter,

"Now go out where it is deeper, and let down your nets to catch some fish." (Luke 5:4) "'Master,' Simon replied, 'we worked hard all last night and didn't catch a thing. But if you say so, I'll let the nets down again.'" (Luke 5:5) The story goes on to say that when Peter let the down the nets again, the fish literally jumped into them so fast and furious that the nets begin to tear, and the boat, along with another that rowed over to help, began to sink! Peter's reaction gives a glimpse into his heart, and it is so powerful because it also reveals something very important about Jesus. Peter fell to his knees and said, "Oh, Lord, please leave me—I'm too much of a sinner to be around you." (Luke 5:8) Jesus' goodness had so overwhelmed him that Peter saw his true nature and that of Jesus as well. This is a beautiful example of Romans 2:4—

> Don't you see how wonderfully kind, tolerant, and patient God is with you? Does this mean nothing to you? Can't you see that his kindness is intended to turn you from your sin?

When we experience the grace of God, His goodness is what leads us to repent—to change our minds and turn in His direction. Isn't that amazing? God's goodness gives us the desire to turn from sin and head straight into His arms, because we realize it is He who is good and He who loves us in the midst of our humanity.

It's not His condemnation or His judgment that leads one to *truly* repent, as I believed before I understood the gospel of grace. It's His kindness that draws us to Him. Just take a look at John 3:16-17. Most people know John 3:16 by heart—"For God so loved the world, that he gave his only begotten Son, that whosoever believeth in him should not perish, but have everlasting life."(KJV) That verse is so important, but we often look right over verse 17, which to me, is equally important. Let's take a look—"For God sent not his Son into the world to *condemn* the world; but that the world through him might be saved." (KJV-emphasis mine) We are saved by grace, not by our own efforts.

His grace is His *unearned, unmerited* favor. And when we depend on ourselves, our own efforts, and our good behavior to qualify us and place us in right standing with Him, we are unable to receive all of His wonderful grace. It has to be ALL Him, or it's simply not grace. Grace is a gift. There is nothing we can do to earn it. Grace is Jesus, and He met every requirement of the law, every requirement we could never meet. He did it all for us, so that we can have complete security, complete peace, complete victory and eternal life in Him!

Peter saw the goodness of Jesus and his own sinful nature, and Jesus didn't disqualify him! No, Jesus still wanted Peter to follow Him and to learn from

Him, and thankfully Peter didn't allow his self-image to get in the way of Jesus' plan to create His own image within Peter. This transformation would take some time.

Peter was most likely with Jesus day and night for three years. He heard the teachings, saw the miracles of restoration and recreation, and even saw the dead raised to life again. He and the other disciples were also sent by Jesus to minister and heal in His name (Luke 9:1-27). And Peter had the privilege of being the first disciple to declare Jesus' true identity. "You are the Christ, the Son of the living God." (Matthew 16:16 NKJV) Jesus then changed his name from Simon to Peter, which means "rock." This rock-solid, enduring revelation of who Jesus is moved Jesus to change Peter's name!

Out of the twelve disciples, Jesus had an inner circle of three, and Peter was in that circle along with James and John. These three men were privy to extremely important conversations and events that the other disciples were not. And all three were known for having hot tempers, impulsive natures, and many other imperfections. This is a clear indication that we must not allow our imperfections to disqualify us from having an intimate relationship with Jesus. His strength is made perfect in our weakness! (2 Corinthians 12:9.)

These three men were there on the Mount of Transfiguration and saw Jesus, in all of His glory, visit with Moses and Elijah. Impulsive Peter sprang into action. He immediately suggested that they build shelters for each of them, which used to sound like a really good idea to me, too, until I looked closely at the context. Peter wanted to *do* something rather than just *be* in the presence of Jesus and see His glory revealed. God intervened to show Peter what was most important by saying from Heaven, "'This is My beloved Son, in whom I am well pleased. *Hear* Him!'" (Matthew 17:5 NKJV- emphasis mine)

The most critical aspect in our quest to grow in the Lord is to *hear* Him. We must spend time in His Word and in prayer—both listening and talking to Him. And the wonderful thing about spending time with God is that under grace it is no longer a chore to be endured but a privilege to be enjoyed! Is there anyone out there like me who read the Bible and threw a few words up to Heaven to mark them off your spiritual to-do list? To be honest, I viewed these things as laborious tasks when I was doing them in my own effort as a way to please God. When I began to *realize* my identity in Christ—as righteous in Him apart from my own effort—and *receive* God's great love for me, I couldn't wait to get in the Word to see what mystery God might reveal to me or to find shadows of Jesus in the Old Testament! The Word began to come alive and speak to my heart in ways of which I had only dreamed. Prayer became a time of sweet fellowship that I didn't want to end. When I shifted my focus from myself and my own efforts and placed it on Jesus and His finished work on the cross, my time with the Lord became a respite instead of a requirement.

Peter began to have an identity transformation as he spent time with Jesus. He went from a rough, hot-tempered fisherman driven by impulsivity to a humble servant of his Savior and his fellow man. One of the things for which Peter is most remembered is his denial of Jesus, not just once but three times. This occurred shortly after his declaration of loyalty to Jesus—even to death if necessary (John 13:37-38). When Jesus was arrested in the Garden of Gethsemane and taken to Caiaphas' courtyard, Peter followed, hanging back in the shadows so as not to be noticed. He needed to be near Jesus but not so near as to be associated with Him. Oh, how I've been there before! On three occasions, Peter was asked about his relationship with Jesus and he denied knowing Him each time, and the last time vehemently. That's when the cock crowed, which Jesus predicted in John 13:38, and Jesus looked at him. Peter was undone. Weeping bitterly, he fled the courtyard thinking that his relationship with Jesus had been severed (Luke 22:54-61).

Here is where I weep, too, because I have been right where Peter was! My tears are empathetic, because I also hid my belief in Jesus before I had a revelation of His grace and His love for me. Remember the Christian cassette tapes concealed in my console? That's one time of many. Have you been there, too? If so, I have good news for you that will wash every bit of guilt away and empower you to walk in boldness and love where your relationship with Jesus is concerned. Here it is— Jesus does not condemn you for it, and He does not relinquish His relationship with you because of it. We see this in what happened for Peter after Jesus' resurrection.

Take a look at Mark 16:7. The angel spoke to the women who came to the tomb on the morning of Jesus' resurrection. They found it empty, and the angel said, "Now go and tell his disciples, *including Peter*, that Jesus is going ahead of you to Galilee. You will see him there, just as he told you before he died.'" (Emphasis mine) The angel mentioned Peter specifically as if to say, "Peter, nothing has changed in your relationship with Jesus. He loves you still! You are not disqualified. You are not condemned. Now all of your sins have been cleansed by His precious blood! Go to Him, Peter. He's waiting for you!" Oh, I get so excited and emotional about this because Jesus is saying the same thing to us today, friend! No, His marvelous grace is not a license to sin as some have erroneously believed. It will not produce more sin as some pastors have erroneously preached. It is His favor that is greater than all our sin (Romans

5:20), and it allows us to receive His love, forgiveness, and gift of no condemnation. His approval empowers us to walk free from sin, and we are approved by His blood when we receive Him as our Lord and Savior.

This was only the beginning for our friend Peter. After the angel's invitation to Galilee, Peter accompanied the other disciples to their old stomping ground to wait for Jesus. I love how Peter's story had come full circle! While they waited, Peter decided to go fishing, and the others joined him. Just as our story began, he heard that familiar voice with the Heavenly timbre call from the shore just as it had years ago. "He called out, 'Fellows, have you caught any fish?'" (John 21:5) That voice that spoke the world into being directed them to cast their nets on the other size, and a haul came in just as it had before. Then they knew. And our dear impulsive Peter, who just could not be constrained, dove in and swam toward the shore like Michael Phelps! Jesus was waiting to receive Him with open arms and breakfast, too.

What a Savior! "For he knows how weak we are; he remembers we are only dust." (Ps. 103:14) He picks up the pieces of our broken lives, loves us into wholeness, and in His presence we are continually fed. In turn, this enables us to walk with the broken, love them as He does, and feed them from the sustenance we receive from Jesus. We can never genuinely accomplish this by ourselves. Only through who we are in Him can we authentically love others. Oh, how I love Him for this!

Alas, this wasn't the end for Peter. It was only the beginning! After Jesus' ascension into Heaven, Peter and the rest of the disciples returned to Jerusalem to wait for the promised Holy Spirit (Acts 2-3). When He came on the day of Pentecost, they received power from on high to become the witnesses that would turn the world upside down! Peter went on to preach Jesus in Jerusalem that very day with great boldness. Just a short time before, he had been hiding in the shadows of that city and following Jesus at a distance. Now he was out in the open, proclaiming Jesus to the masses! Three thousand people believed in Jesus that day and were saved. Later we find Peter and John on the Temple Mount at the Beautiful Gate healing a lame man then proclaiming Jesus again in the Temple. Talk about boldness! Peter's identity had truly been transformed by His Savior, and he spent the rest of his earthly life following in Jesus' footsteps and catching people for Him.

Chapter 5—Identifying God as Father

Anyone who knows my daddy knows that he is not about to allow anyone to hurt his girls. My sister, Christy, and I grew up with the security of our daddy as stalwart protector. We felt completely safe in his presence. Daddy told us he loved us every day as he headed off to work to provide for our family.

If anything needed repairing or building, my daddy was the man for the job, or if trouble arose, he was ready to defend. I remember one such time of trouble back in the 1970s when I was about five years old. An arsonist was stalking our sleepy community that summer, and the scariest part for me was that he disguised himself as a werewolf. His MO was to throw homemade explosives into the front windows of houses that lined our quiet streets. He would then stand back in the shadows and watch them burn.

One night I remember being particularly afraid because Daddy and our neighbor Earl had decided to keep watch on our front porch in case the werewolf struck our street. I was so afraid that he would get my daddy! As I grew older, I saw Daddy's immense love for us in keeping watch that night outside my window, keeping all the bad guys at bay. Daddy would allow nothing harmful to come near us if it was within his power.

Isn't that just like our Heavenly Father? Our Daddy God continually keeps watch over us, and *it is* within His power to always keep harm from us. Psalm 121:4 assures us that God never sleeps.

And the werewolf in my narrative is a snapshot of the devil—disguising himself to invoke greater fear and stalking in darkness, hiding in shadows to watch his fires bring our lives to ruins. But our Abba, our Daddy God, is ever watchful and hides us under His wings (Psalm 91).

Before the revelation of grace, I had a very difficult time seeing God as a good Father. I easily saw Him as harsh, stern, and virtually unapproachable. Like many other Christians, I had mistaken the true identity of my Father. About a year into my grace journey—knowing that I had been made right with God by his gift of grace and not my own efforts—I began to ask Him to show me His true identity. According to my new understanding, I knew in my heart that I had Him all wrong. I knew that Jesus— God, the Son—loved me because of His sacrifice on the cross, but I was still finding it difficult to believe that God the Father did. I never considered how much love it required for Him to give up His beloved Son for me. How many parents would give up their dearly loved child for a good person let alone a sinner? None I know. It took fathomless love for our Father to give His Son with no guarantee that we would accept His gift. 1 John 4:10 conveys it so clearly: "This is real love—not that we loved God, but that he loved us and sent his Son as a sacrifice to take away our sins."

I began to pray and ask God to reveal His love for me. Almost immediately, I began to sense that love, and He took me to His Word and reminded me of the words of Jesus. Jesus said that anyone who had seen Him had seen the Father (John 14:9). Jesus spoke these words to His disciple Philip, who asked Jesus to show him and the other disciples the Father. Jesus' response was that He was a perfect representation of Him!

Many of my misconceptions about God as Father stemmed from what I saw in the Old Testament—also known as the old covenant—before Jesus made a way to restore us to the Father. As the Holy Spirit has revealed the true nature of God to me over these last four years, I've come to the profound understanding of His goodness and His holiness and that we, in ourselves, are neither. God is a just God. His ways—His standards—are perfect, and we are not, thus our inability to maintain them in our own efforts.

In the opening chapter of this book, we discovered how Adam's sin had to be sentenced because of God's judiciousness. Sin's wage is death according to Romans 6:23. There had to be a payment, an atoning for Adam's sin. The atonement for death is life. Our life force is blood. Without blood, we cannot live. Therefore, God instituted the blood sacrifice. An innocent's blood for the guilty, the exchange made for the transgressor to live and find forgiveness from God. Under the old system of animal sacrifice, the forgiveness was temporary. Under our new and better covenant of Jesus' sacrifice, the forgiveness is eternal!

Before the fall, Adam and Eve were crowned and clothed with the glory of God their Father. They enjoyed sweet fellowship with Him continually. When they fell, God's great love for them made the first sacrifice of an innocent animal, covered their nakedness, and sent them away from the garden to ensure their inaccessibility to the tree of life and to set in motion His redemptive plan that would culminate in Jesus' own sacrifice some 4,000 years later.

Fast forward to the time of Moses and the children of Israel in captivity in Egypt. After nine attempts— nine plagues—to secure their release, God instructed Moses to institute the first Passover (Exodus 12). The children of Israel were to put the blood of a spotless lamb on the doorposts of their homes. They were to stay inside and partake of the Passover meal, which included the lamb, because God was going to send the death angel, whose actions would ultimately gain their freedom from Egypt and Pharaoh.

That night as the Jewish people partook of the lamb safely hidden under the blood on their doorposts, the death angel passed over. For those who did not apply the blood to their doorposts, the firstborn of each family died, including Pharaoh's own son. He finally agreed to allow the Israelites to go free.

Forty years later we see Israel enter the Promised Land. God promised them His very best if they would obey His commands and follow His provision for the covering of their sins through the sacrificial system He instituted in the wilderness. Alas, after they entered in and enjoyed victory after victory over their enemies and all of the blessings of God's provision, they turned to the idols their neighbors worshiped. They sacrificed on the hilltops and under the trees just as the pagans did. They sacrificed animals and sometimes their own children, which broke God's heart and kindled His anger. They were double-minded and wanted to worship God and idols. As Proverbs 20:10 declares, God despises double standards of any type. This includes our own double-mindedness (James 1:8). Either we trust Him, or we don't. There is no in-between. In Exodus 20:3, God commanded that the Israelites were to have no other gods before Him. He alone was to be worshiped. Jesus plainly tells us in Matthew 6:24 that "No one can serve two masters. For you will hate one and love the other; you will be devoted to one and despise the other. . ."

History tells us that each time the Israelites fell into idol worship, the blood sacrifice for atonement was either ignored or practiced along with other sacrifices. Thus, there was nothing to assuage the wrath of our holy God. Today we so often see rules being bent and standards being removed for the more popular "do what's right for you" mentality. God doesn't change even though our culture and mindsets do. He is still holy, and sin still requires a payment. Praise the name of Jesus, because He is the overpayment for our sin! Because of Jesus and His shed blood, we now live under the grace and the mercy of our loving Father. God hasn't changed from the Old to the New Testament, even though it may appear as though He has. The only thing that has changed is that a perfect sacrifice has been made, one that will last through all eternity because Jesus, the Lamb of God, gave His own life as a ransom for ours. The sin wage has been paid, and the enemy has been defeated. The blood is God's provision for sinful man's atonement. Jesus was born under the law to fulfill all of the law's requirements. His sacrifice satisfied the wrath of God for all time. Jesus bore the wrath and the excruciating pain of separation from His Father so that we can incur God's tremendous love and favor and enjoy an intimate, endless relationship with Him. Jesus has made God our Father, too.

Our Father is love. We see this over and over in the Scriptures. John 3:16 assures us that "For God loved the world so much that he gave his one and only Son, so that everyone who believes in him will not perish but have eternal life." 1 John 4:16 says, "We know how much God loves us, and we have put our trust in His love. God is love, and all who live in love live in God, and God lives in them." 1 John 4:18-19 go on to say that

> Such love has no fear, because perfect love expels all fear. If we are afraid, it is for fear of punishment, and this shows that we have not fully experienced his perfect love. We love each other because he loved us first.

And Psalm 103:11 promises, "For his unfailing love toward those who fear him is as great as the height of the heavens above the earth."

We live in a fallen world, and often people blame God for the atrocities and catastrophes that surround us. They don't really know or even consider that when Adam sinned, he relinquished the authority, the dominion over the earth, which was given to him by God. When he yielded to Satan, Adam gave Satan his authority, whereby Satan is now called "the god of this world" (2 Corinthians 4:4). He comes to steal, kill, and destroy (John 10:10). The destruction we see is caused by him. He is the thief, the murderer, and the destroyer. God is a good Father! He sent Jesus to give His life so that we can have an abundant life overflowing with His goodness. If my earthly, imperfect father wants the very best for his daughters, how much more our Heavenly Father, our Abba, our Daddy God! Oh, friend, see Him as Daddy!

Seeing God this way can be very difficult for those who've had abusive or absent fathers or for those who've been abandoned. Abba, Daddy God, wants to heal the hurts that earthly fathers have inflicted. We can run to Him as His beloved sons and daughters and receive His love! I do this on a frequent basis. I thank Him for loving me and then say something like this, "Abba, I receive Your love for me today. I thank You that it covers my heart by the power of the Holy Spirit. I receive Your love, and I can give it out to other people." When we know that we are deeply loved by God, we can love others and love them well without fear.

I encourage you, dear reader, to ask God to reveal Himself to you as Abba. He *will* reveal Himself to you. If you have issues from your past—hurts that won't seem to heal, memories that paralyze you with fear or grip you with pain—Abba will make all things new. I know this from personal experience. The sexual abuse I endured as a child left me with a great deal of guilt, shame, and anxiety. I had nightmares about my abuser until well into my twenties. They progressed into night terrors that were really demonic episodes that paralyzed me in my sleep and left me clawing my way back to consciousness, often waking myself with muffled screams. Ever since I began to understand my right standing with God based on Jesus' finished work and to receive Abba's love for me, the night terrors have completely vanished, and all the pain from the memories of the abuse has been washed away. When I think of my childhood now, I rarely ever think of the abuse. When do I remember, it's as if it never happened to me. The love of my Father, through the finished work of Jesus, has disarmed it and stripped it of all its ability to hurt me or bring me shame (Colossians 2:14-15). How great is His love for me and for you!

There is a childhood memory that I recently revisited, and I believe that it truly conveys Abba's heart for me. Back in the 1970s , my family loved to eat at a restaurant called Bonanza. I always thought I might see Hoss or Little Joe from that classic TV series of the same name when I went there, so a culinary outing to Bonanza was high on my list! The restaurant had the best steaks and hamburgers in town, but the big draw for me was the cubed Jell-O in the fancy dessert dish with a dollop of whipped cream. The only thing that troubled me about my favorite restaurant was the paneled half wall which held the queue in check as it wound around to the serving counter. It was super high to a four-year-old and utterly dark below it. On one of our dinner outings, I found myself walking beside my parents and becoming lost in that darkness and a sea of bell-bottoms as we meandered behind the partition. I can still remember how dark it was down there, and I can still feel the trepidation in my little heart as I tugged on Daddy's pant leg. "Hey! It's dark down here!" I cried. Daddy instantly looked down and saw my plight. There was his tow-headed, pigtailed little girl way down in that abyss of polyester! He instantly lifted me into His arms, up into the light, and held me close to his heart. "Now, that's better!" he chuckled.

This has always been one of my favorite memories, but lately when I recall it, I am moved to tears because I see my Heavenly Father so clearly in it. He sees us in our darkness, and moved with compassion by our cries, He lifts us into His arms, up into the light, and holds us close to His heart. We're secure in Daddy's arms and in His love. And it is so much better! This is our Father, friend! I pray that you will know and receive His love for you. It surpasses our comprehension, yet it floods our understanding with who He really is. He's a good, good Father, and you are so very precious to Him.

In the stories we've recalled, Peter's touches my heart most deeply. I can truly empathize with him because I've been the hot-tempered one, putting my husband out at the entrance to our subdivision *on a Sunday on our way home from church* because I was infuriated with him and now can't even remember why. It must have been really important! I've been the one who was so jealous of others and the blessings that came their way. I think Peter was jealous of his contemporary John in many ways, as I've heard several teachers expound upon. I, too, have been worried about my position and my own needs just as Peter was.

I've depended on my own efforts and almost burst with pride when I did well (in my estimation) or drank the dregs of despair when I had missed the mark. I've denied knowing the Lord by remaining silent at certain times, and I have been embarrassed and afraid, hoping others wouldn't see me as a religious nut. But just like Peter, that was before I truly understood what Jesus' life and death mean for me.

When the revelation of my true identity—that my righteousness is rooted in Christ instead of myself—became my reality, I was a life changed forever, and now I just can't stop telling people about how wonderful Jesus is! Please don't misunderstand; I still have days where I miss the mark. Every day I drive a car on the highway and interact with people, and both activities offer a variety of opportunities for some old-nature antics!

I don't always agree with my husband or other family members, and I still fall short because I am human. The big difference is that right in the middle of any old-nature actions or inclinations, I can still say and believe that I am "a new person. The old life is gone; a new life has begun!" (2 Corinthians 5:17) I now say, "I'm sorry, Lord," out of a sincere heart and move on. Before, I would have stayed mired in guilt and condemnation for days, maybe weeks depending on the severity of my misbehavior, until I could clean myself up. Just how I expected to do that is still a mystery to me. Depending on Jesus and Him alone has brought such clarity and peace to my life. I am by no means perfect, but I belong to a Savior who is!

According to God's Word, I am righteous because of the finished work of Jesus (2 Corinthians 5:21). As I focus on Jesus and His finished work, my behavior will parallel my identity in Him. Right in the midst of wrong behavior, I can proclaim my identity in Christ by saying, "I am the righteousness of God in Christ Jesus."

To our natural minds, a simple confession doesn't hold much power. But God uses simple things to confound the wise (I Corinthians 1:27), and what you say about yourself is powerful. I encourage you to keep making a right confession until you see right results. I am a life that has been changed by changing my beliefs about how to be made right with God and by changing what I say about myself.

I've already told you some of my story, but I really want to share some of the immense changes that have been wrought in my life over the last four years. One of the greatest changes is becoming free of fear. My mother might as well have named me Phobia because you name it, and I was afraid of it. Being home alone, heights, clowns, oxygen deprivation, contracting sicknesses that I heard or I read about, darkness, storms, snakes, people, and rejection are just a sampling! I am now walking free of fear because of the love my Father has for me. One of my favorite Scriptures is 2 Timothy 1:7 (KJV): "For God hath not given us the spirit of fear; but of power, and of love, and of a sound mind." Since God doesn't give fear, that totally exposes the one who does! When we know fear is not of God and that we are deeply loved by Him, the fear melts away, and God's power, love, and peace of mind become our reality.

The first fears from which I was delivered were those of being home alone at night and of being in the dark. Even as a teenager, I would sleep in my parents' room on occasion because my fear was so intense. After my husband Mike and I were married, and he began to travel, I would spend the night at my parents' house and make sure I was there before dark because I was so terrified of being in the house alone. About a year ago, packing my stuff and spending the night away from home during the week began to wear on me. I teach elementary school, and goodness knows I need all the rest I can get! Can I get an *"Amen,"* teacher friends? A little alone time doesn't hurt either.

One Wednesday night, as Mike was preparing to go out of town, I decided that I would stay at home while he was away. After all, I was a big girl of 45 and could surely brave the night alone even if I stayed awake and watched TV, which was initially my plan. I kissed Mike goodbye that Thursday morning, went on to school, and made sure I got home before dark. I decided to sleep on the sofa in the living room so that I could have a better view of my surroundings. I left the TV on and slept fitfully, but I stayed home! I was thrilled! This became my pattern for his next few trips.

Then one night I thought, "I've got that big comfy bed one room away. Why am I sleeping on this sofa?" I headed to my room and climbed into bed. I turned out all the lights (major step!), thanked the Lord for keeping me safe while I slept, and had one of the best night's sleeps I've ever had! It's now been over a year, and I actually enjoy that "alone" time. I'm never really alone because Jesus is always with me, and it's uninterrupted time that I get to spend with Him.

Fear is a harsh taskmaster. It is debilitating and unyielding, but when the perfect love of God becomes a reality in the believer's life, fear has no choice but to flee from the One who gave His life to free us from it.

God has also delivered me from my fear of people and rejection, which stemmed from my deep insecurity. Growing up, I was always very timid and shy. As I mentioned earlier, I wouldn't even place takeout orders or talk with anyone over the phone other than my family and friends. I was so afraid I would make a mistake or sound dumb. I often avoided eye contact with people when I was out because I was painfully self-conscious. If someone was laughing, the laughter had to be directed at me. My intrinsic focus robbed me of peace and joy and led me down a road of self-loathing. I found it extremely difficult to talk to people at times because of my self-consciousness. Now that I am Jesus-conscious, I look forward to talking to people and even seek them out to try to find inroads to talk to them about Jesus.

Another fear in my menagerie was that of snakes. Can I get a witness? I was terrified of snakes, and I still don't like them that much, but the sight of them no longer petrifies me. I used to shake uncontrollably and feel nauseated when I saw a snake in a book or on TV, let alone in real life. Over the last two years, I have encountered more snakes than in my other 44 years combined! Here's the cool thing, though—every snake I have come across has either been dead, dying, or slithering away at the sight of me! The latter occurred when I "outed" a copperhead in the line of folks waiting to ride the train at the Birmingham Zoo. By "outed," I mean shouted, "Snake!" My old fearful self would probably have tried to climb into the stroller with the baby beside me, but my renewed self stood her ground and watched that fellow slither back from whence he came!

After several of these strange occurrences regarding snakes, I began to hear the Lord speaking to me about them. He reminded me that I had been praying Psalm 91 over myself and my family every day. Verse 13 says, "You will trample upon lions and cobras; you will crush fierce lions and serpents under your feet!" I got so excited when He revealed that to me! In confessing God's promises over my life, I was seeing the manifestation in the natural. He reminded me that though I might see them, those snakes were powerless to hurt me because He had already dealt with them before I saw them in my path. What a good, good Father! He goes before us and makes our way clear!

My freedom from fear stems from this truth: ". . . perfect love expels *all* fear." (1 John 4:18-emphasis mine). When I began to *realize* and *receive* my Father's perfect love for me, all my fears began to wash away under the torrent of that love. If you are dealing with fear of any kind, I encourage you to begin to confess, "My Father loves me perfectly, and His perfect love takes away my fear." I believe that you will begin to experience freedom as you change what you say and the way you believe about our Father's love. It is boundless, unconditional, and liberating!

Not only has God's love enabled me to walk away from fear, but it has also enabled me to love myself and others. As I'm sure you can see, I was really a mess, but, again, I was no surprise to my Father. When Mike and I married, I was so insecure that it was very difficult for me to hear any criticism, much less receive it and learn from it. Mike also had a lot of insecurities. A house with two insecure people is like a mine field. It is a tricky business indeed to have to tiptoe around each other, because sooner or later someone is going to trip the wire and an explosion of mass proportions will ensue. God's grace has done such a healing work in our marriage. There is a tenderness and security that has been birthed in both of us by God alone. I am now able and willing to say that I'm sorry and to ask for forgiveness when I have hurt Mike, and he is able to do the same. I am also able to grant forgiveness, whereas I used to take a degree of pleasure in withholding it.

The love we have for each other now is deeper and stronger than ever before because it is rooted in God's love for us as individuals. When you love your spouse out of the reservoir of the Father's love in you, it's a healing balm that will restore both of you. This is our promise that the reservoir indeed resides within all of us who have been born again—"And this hope will not lead to disappointment. For we know how dearly God loves us, because he has given us the Holy Spirit to fill our hearts with his love." (Romans 5:5) This is one of my favorite Scriptures to pray because I need to remind myself of God's love in me so that I can receive it and give it out to others.

In Christ we really have been given everything that pertains to *life* and *godliness* (2 Peter 1:3 KJV-emphasis mine). If the enemy can keep us from accessing our inheritance in Christ by masking our identity with our own efforts, guilt, and condemnation, he can keep us defeated, weak, and quiet. When we know who we are in Christ, we become limitless because it's Christ who empowers us to live right. He gives us His strength, and we have access to all that He is and all that He died to give us by being found in Him. The way we are found in Him is by believing in Him. The miracles that He did "are written so that you may continue to believe that Jesus is the Messiah, the Son of God, and that by believing in him you will have life by the power of his name." (John 20:31)

The simple truth is that God loves you, and He loves me beyond our comprehension. So great is His love for us that He allowed His beloved Son to be crucified in our stead; to die a criminal's death that we deserved; and to *judiciously and completely* save us from eternal death and Hell itself. God is a just God, and His fiery judgment fell on His Son. Through Jesus' sacrifice, His wrath toward our sin was satisfied. God will not judge the same crime twice. Mankind's treason that was perpetrated in the Garden of Eden was judged on the cross. When we accept Jesus as our Savior, when we believe in Him, we stand sinless under the continually cleansing flow of His blood. *All* of our sins—past, present, and future—have been judged at the cross (Colossians 2:13). We no longer confess our sin *to be forgiven*. We confess our sin *because we are forgiven*! And that makes all the difference. Jesus' blood speaks (Hebrews 12:24). For 2,000 years and into eternity it cries, "Finished! Forgiven! Righteous! Redeemed!" This is our true identity in Him!

Chapter 7-*How to Find Your Identity in Christ*

My primary goal in writing this book is to help believers understand who they are in Christ, but if you've never invited Jesus into your life, nothing would thrill me more than to tell you how to do just that and to help you understand all that Jesus has done and wants to do for you. My ultimate goal in all things, including the writing of this book, is to glorify Jesus and lift Him high so that people will be drawn to Him and have life in His name.

My friend, if you've never met this wonderful Savior, you can find your true identity in Him, and all you have to do is believe on Him and confess that belief as you invite Him into your heart with this simple prayer. He will hear you, and He will save you. Pray this from your heart:

> "Jesus, I believe in You. I believe that You are God's Son and that you died for me and rose again. I turn from my sins, and I confess You as my Lord. I know that my sins are all forgiven—past, present, and future—and that I am forever cleansed by Your blood. I receive Your love and Your grace for me today. In Jesus' Name. Amen."

If you prayed that prayer, you are born again of the Spirit of God, a new creation, and God's own son or daughter. I rejoice with you! Go tell somebody about it!

As our time together comes to a close, I'd like to briefly expound on what I mean by the gospel of grace, law and grace, and the old covenant and new covenant. These terms have been used throughout the preceding chapters, and no one can explain them better than the Apostle Paul, to whom Jesus Himself ministered these principles. In Romans 3:19-31, Paul differentiates between the law that was given to Moses and the grace of God which came by Jesus Christ:

> Obviously, the law applies to those to whom it was given, *for its purpose is to keep people from having excuses, and to show that the entire world is guilty before God. For no one can ever be made right with God by doing what the law commands. The law simply shows us how sinful we are.*
> But now God has shown us a way to be made right with him without keeping the requirements of the law, as was promised in the writings of Moses and the prophets long ago. *We are made right with God by placing our faith in Jesus Christ. And this is true for everyone who believes, no matter who we are.*
> For everyone has sinned; we all fall short of God's glorious standard. *Yet God, with*

underserved kindness, declares that we are righteous. He did this through Christ Jesus when he freed us from the penalty for our sins. For God presented Jesus as the sacrifice for sin. *People are made right with God when they believe that Jesus sacrificed His life, shedding His blood.* This sacrifice shows that God was being fair when He held back and did not punish those who sinned in times past, for he was looking ahead and including them in what he would do in the present time. *God did this to demonstrate his righteousness, for he himself is fair and just, and he declares sinners to be right in his sight when they believe in Jesus. Can we boast, then, that we have done anything to be accepted by God? No, because our acquittal is not based on obeying the law. It is based on faith. So we are made right with God through faith and not by obeying the law.* After all, is God the God of the Jews only? Isn't he also the God of the Gentiles? Of course he is. There is only one God, and he makes people right with himself only by faith, whether they are Jews or Gentiles. Well then, if we emphasize faith, does this mean that we can forget about the law? Of course not! In fact, only when

we have faith do we truly fulfill the law.
(Emphasis mine)

Do you see what Paul is getting at here in the last
verse? He is making it clear that we are not made
right with God by keeping the law—the Ten
Commandments and the myriad of other
regulations that the Israelites lived under, which in
truth numbered upward of 600. Only when we
have faith in Jesus can we keep it. He empowers us
to do the right thing when we trust in Him and not
in ourselves. The law was given to show that we
cannot keep God's perfect standard. God never
intended for the law to save us. If it could, then
Jesus would have died in vain. God, in His great
love, sent His Son, who was all God and all man.
Jesus kept the law perfectly and then gave His life,
just as a spotless, sacrificial lamb was given for sin
under the law. His perfect blood, His God blood
was the requirement to wash *all* our sin away—
past, present, and future—forever! I now know
that it's not my confession of sin that makes me
right with God, as I used to believe. Don't
misunderstand. That doesn't mean I just go on my
merry way, doing as I please, never acknowledging
when I sin. In fact, nothing could be further from
the truth. I know when I sin, and I am quick to say,
"Oh, Lord, I'm so sorry. Thank You for Your
forgiveness and for Your blood that continually
cleanses me! I am righteous in You and You alone,
Jesus."

Before I understood the complete forgiveness I have in Christ, I would inwardly beat myself to pieces and live under a load of guilt and condemnation. I was always trying to clean myself up and live perfectly in my own effort. I was worn out, defeated, and almost always certain that I wasn't really saved. I was trying to save myself and add to Jesus' *finished* work on the cross.

Have you ever wondered why Jesus cried, "It is finished!" right before he died (John 19:30)? I have. And now I know. It's because our salvation, our healing, our deliverance, our redemption, and our right standing with God was complete through the shedding of His perfect blood. There's nothing we can add to it with our works or behavior *or* take away from it with our works or behavior. Now *that* will set you free!

When you are born again, you are a new creation in Christ, even if you don't see a change immediately. Just continue in His Word, continue to hear the gospel of grace, let Him love you into wholeness, and you will see the change inwardly and outwardly. Just let go of who you are in your own efforts and receive your new identity *in Christ!*

In order to grow in the Lord and in your new identity, I encourage you to find a Bible translation that you can understand and read it each day. A great place to start is in the Gospel of John. Begin to talk to God just like you talk to your dearest friend. You can be real and honest with Him. Receive His love daily. During my daily time with God, I like to say out loud, "Father, I receive Your love for me today." Then I take the time to meditate on Jesus.

Get some powerful praise and worship that is Jesus-centered. My friend Sandra shared that she made a "God Loves Me" playlist. It's filled with songs that enable her to feel and receive the Father's love for her. I followed suit and have one, too. I love receiving my Father's love through song.

Make sure you find a grace-based church that is Jesus-centered and where His finished work is preached. My family and I prayed for a grace church for two years, and God has recently led us to it. I am so thankful that my pastor magnifies Jesus and His finished work!

Listen to Jesus-centered teaching on TV and online. My pastor, Brandon Ball, of Church Unlimited in Birmingham, AL, preaches the truth of who Jesus is and who we are in Him with clarity and humor. I invite you to download the church's app at Church Unlimited Alabama, go to the website www.mychurchunlimited.com where you can listen to all the archived sermons and watch the livestream on Sundays at 9 am and 11 am CST. You will grow and be blessed by the revelation of Jesus and His goodness.

Oh, friend, I conclude our time together with such joy in my heart, trusting God that the truth that has come alive in my heart is now springing to life in yours by the power of the Holy Spirit! Much love to you! Please know that you are in my heart and in my prayers as you experience the awesome goodness of our God. Until we meet again in the pages of another book about our Savior, may our Father bless you with His perfect peace as you experience the riches of His grace in Christ Jesus our Lord. To Him be glory forever!

About the Author

Amy Holmes has a passion for Jesus and for the message of His grace to be made known to all people. Her desire is for believers to understand all that Jesus' finished work on the cross has accomplished and to be able to walk in the fullness thereof.

As an elementary school teacher, Amy's goal is to instill in her students the joy of learning. As a Bible study leader and student of the Word herself, her goal is the same—to instill joy in the learner through unveiling the person of Jesus Christ, all that He is, and all that we can be in Him.

Amy lives in Chelsea, Alabama, with her husband Mike. They have been married for twenty-five years and love traveling and spending time together with family.

Amy cherishes the opportunity to share her story of freedom in Christ with others. She can be contacted via email at amyholmes555@gmail.com.

References

The Every Day Life Bible, Amplified Version.

New York: Faith Words, 2006.

The Holy Bible, King James Version.

New York: Thomas Nelson & Sons.

The Holy Bible, New King James Version.

Nashville: Holman Bible Publishers, 2013.

The Holy Bible, New Living Translation.

Carol Stream: Tyndale House Publishers,

2007.